W9-AZO-470

—A—
CAT
LOVER'S
JOURNAL

Compiled by Bruce W. Currie

PETER PAUPER PRESS, INC.
WHITE PLAINS · NEW YORK

*For my wife Alice
and my cat Cosmo*

Copyright © 1992
Peter Pauper Press, Inc.
202 Mamaroneck Avenue
White Plains, NY 10601
ISBN 0-88088-701-X
Printed in Hong Kong
7 6 5 4 3 2

Admirers of felines—here's your opportunity to record your thoughts in a very special Cat Lover's Journal. These reflections may show you how your life is truly intertwined with that furry little delight.

Naturally, other musings and experiences of everyday life may be noted, such as your feelings toward the current love in your life (*probably* that purr-fect cat). Or maybe you will want to mention a real troublemaker in your midst (certainly *could* be the cat). Or you could complain about that annoying neighbor who cries at night (good chance it *is* the cat).

Do feel free to write whatever comes to your mind. Life is too interesting to let it pass by without some kind of record. (And remember: your cat keeps *its* own diary in a <u>cat</u>-a log).

B.W.C.

Every cat I've known has had a distinct personality.
Unmistakably. I've never known two cats even vaguely alike.

AMY TAUBIN

*I call my kittens Shall and Will
because no one can tell them apart.*

CHRISTOPHER MORLEY

American families are smaller than they once were.
So they simply replaced Sis with a cat.

KATHLEEN FURY

_____

_____

_____

_____

_____

_____

_____

_____

_____

_____

_____

_____

_____

_____

_____

_____

_____

_____

_____

_____

_____

_____

_____

_____

_____

_____

To err is human
To purr feline.
ROBERT BYRNE

Nothing's more determined than a cat on a tin roof —
is there? Is there, baby?

TENNESSEE WILLIAMS,
Cat on a Hot Tin Roof

No matter how much cats fight,
there always seem to be plenty of kittens.

ABRAHAM LINCOLN

A cat in despondency sighed,
And resolved to commit suicide;
She passed under the wheels
Of eight automobiles,
And after the ninth one she died.

A cat can be trusted to purr when she is pleased,
which is more than can be said for human beings.

WILLIAM RALPH INGE

Why so lean, my lady cat?
Is it fasting causes that?
Say, or is it love?

MATSUO BASHO

*Did you hear about the cat who ate cheese
and waited by the mouse hole with baited breath?*

A cat also has nine wives.

EVAN ESAR

A cat licking herself solves most of the problems of infection.
We wash too much and finally it kills us.

WILLIAM CARLOS WILLIAMS

A kitten does not discover that her tail belongs to her
until you tread upon it.

HENRY DAVID THOREAU

_____

_____

_____

_____

_____

_____

_____

_____

_____

_____

_____

_____

_____

_____

_____

_____

_____

_____

_____

_____

_____

_____

To escort a cat abroad on a leash
is against the nature of the cat . . .

ADLAI STEVENSON

If man could be crossed with the cat it would improve man,
but it would deteriorate the cat.

MARK TWAIN

_____

_____

_____

_____

_____

_____

_____

_____

_____

_____

_____

_____

_____

_____

_____

_____

_____

_____

_____

_____

_____

_____

_____

_____

If a dog jumps up into your lap, it is because he is fond of you;
but if a cat does the same thing, it is because your lap is warmer.

ALFRED NORTH WHITEHEAD

God made the cat in order that man might have the pleasure of caressing the tiger.

FERNAND MERY

Cats seem to go on the principle that it never does any harm
to ask for what you want.

JOSEPH WOOD KRUTCH

_____

_____

_____

_____

_____

_____

_____

_____

_____

_____

_____

_____

_____

_____

_____

_____

_____

_____

_____

_____

_____

_____

_____

_____

_____

_____

_____

*Of all God's creatures there is only one
that cannot be made the slave of the lash.
That one is the cat.*

MARK TWAIN

It is better to be a mouse in a cat's mouth
than a man in a lawyer's hands.

SPANISH PROVERB

The way to keep a cat is to try to chase it away.

ED HOWE

Walking . . . is a distasteful form of exercise to a cat unless he has a purpose in view.

CARL VAN VECHTEN

Cats are smarter than dogs.
You can't get eight cats to pull a sled through snow.

JEFF VALDEZ

Cats, incidentally, are a great warm-up for a successful marriage —
they teach you your place in the household.

PAUL GALLICO

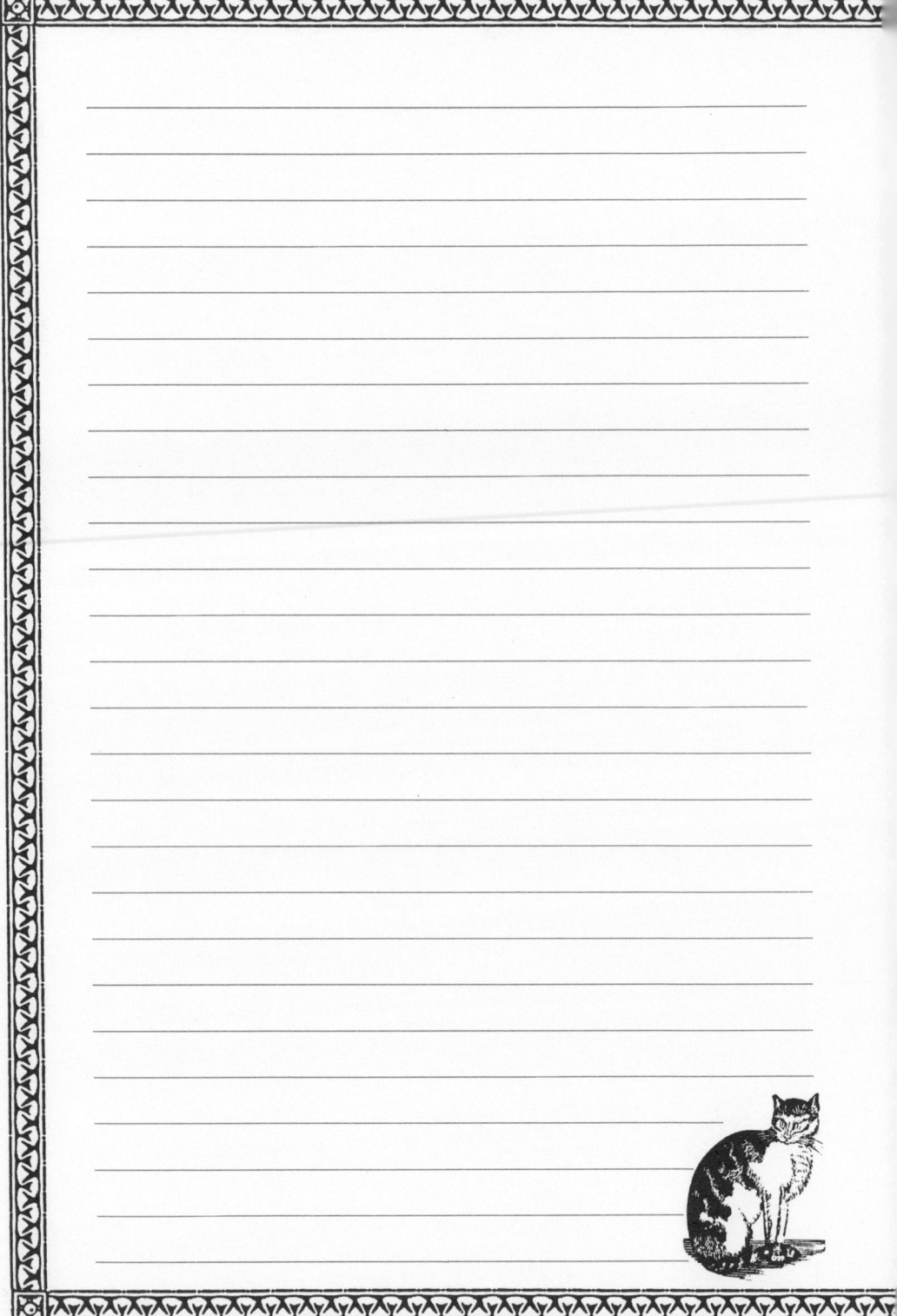

*When I play with my cat,
who knows whether I do not make her
more sport than she makes me?*

MICHEL DE MONTAIGNE

*The difference between Papa and Mamma is that
Mamma loves morals and Papa loves cats.*

MARK TWAIN'S DAUGHTER SUSY

A cat pent up becomes a lion.

ITALIAN PROVERB

A cat dreams all night long of a sheep's tail.

PERSIAN PROVERB

Dogs come when they're called;
cats take a message and get back to you.

MARY BLY

Cats . . . can read your character
better than a $50 an hour psychiatrist.

PAUL GALLICO

_____

_____

_____

_____

_____

_____

_____

_____

_____

_____

_____

_____

_____

_____

_____

_____

_____

_____

_____

_____

_____

_____

_____

_____

A cat is the only domestic animal I know
who toilet trains itself and does a damned impressive job of it.

JOSEPH EPSTEIN

Cats at firesides live luxuriously and are the picture of comfort.

LEIGH HUNT

Throw a cat over a house and it will land on its feet.

ENGLISH PROVERB

_____

_____

_____

_____

_____

_____

_____

_____

_____

_____

_____

_____

_____

_____

_____

_____

_____

_____

_____

_____

_____

_____

_____

_____

Did St. Francis preach to the birds? Whatever for? If he really liked birds he would have done better to preach to the cats.

REBECCA WEST

A cat is a snake in furs.
EDITH WHARTON

_I have noticed that what cats most appreciate in a human being
is not the ability to produce food which they take for granted —
but his or her entertainment value._

GEOFFREY HOUSEHOLD

A cat, I realize, cannot be everyone's cup of fur.

JOSEPH EPSTEIN

I never heard of one [cat] who suffered from insomnia.

JOSEPH WOOD KRUTCH

Authors are sometimes like tomcats:
they distrust all the other toms, but they are kind to kittens.

MALCOLM COWLEY

I don't mind a cat, in its place.
But its place is not in the middle of my back at 4 a.m.

MAYNARD GOOD STODDARD

_____

_____

_____

_____

_____

_____

_____

_____

_____

_____

_____

_____

_____

_____

_____

_____

_____

_____

_____

_____

_____

_____

_____

*Am writing an essay on the life-history of insects and have abandoned
the idea of writing on "How Cats Spend their Time."*

W.N.P. BARBELLION

*It often happens that a man is more humanely related
to a cat or dog than to any human being.*

HENRY DAVID THOREAU

Cats are living adornments.

EDWIN LENT

The cat in gloves catches no mice.

BENJAMIN FRANKLIN

A cat may go to a monastery,
but she still remains a cat!

AFRICAN PROVERB